A QUICK PRI[MER FOR]
PRACTICING M[ANAGERS]

ORGANIZATIONAL CULTURE

• what • why • how

Ajit Mathur

notionpress.com

INDIA • SINGAPORE • MALAYSIA

Notion Press

Old No. 38, New No. 6
McNichols Road, Chetpet
Chennai - 600 031

First Published by Notion Press 2019
Copyright © Ajit Mathur 2019
All Rights Reserved.

ISBN 978-1-68466-866-3

This book has been published with all efforts taken to make the material error-free after the consent of the author. However, the author and the publisher do not assume and hereby disclaim any liability to any party for any loss, damage, or disruption caused by errors or omissions, whether such errors or omissions result from negligence, accident, or any other cause.

No part of this book may be used, reproduced in any manner whatsoever without written permission from the author, except in the case of brief quotations embodied in critical articles and reviews.

Dedicated with love to...

My late parents

who taught me the value of "values"

Contents

Preface ix

PART 1: WHAT IS ORGANIZATIONAL CULTURE? 1

1.1 What is Organizational Culture? 2
1.2 What Does Culture Look like if Dissected? 4
1.3 What Comes First—Strategy or Culture? 8
1.4 What Does an Enabling Culture Look Like? 10
1.5 Who Decides What Culture We Need? 12
1.6 Is It Beneficial to Involve All the Employees in Deciding the Values of an Organization? 14
1.7 What if We Don't Have a Written Document on Culture? 18
1.8 Is There One "Right" Culture That Every Organization Should Aim to Imbibe? 20
1.9 Is Culture a Constant Regardless of the Progress and Growth of an Organization? 22
1.10 What Are the Key Ingredients of Culture? 24
1.11 What Is a Worthy Mission? 28
1.12 What Do the Core Values and Values *Really* Represent? Are They Different? 30

1.13	What Is the Role of Values in a Day-To-Day Job?	32
1.14	Do Values Evolve Over Time?	34
1.15	How to Convert Values into Actionable Behavior?	36
1.16	What Is the ROI on a Culture Change Program?	38
1.17	Who Owns the Culture? Who Are the Key Stakeholders?	40
1.18	What Is the Board's Role in Shaping Cultural Agenda?	42

Exercise 1: Your Organization's Culture—a Quick Assessment 44

PART 2: WHY DOES ORGANIZATIONAL CULTURE MATTER? 49

2.1	Why Does Culture Matter?	50
2.2	We Are Successful—Why Should We Care about Culture?	52
2.3	Can Different Parts of the Same Organization Have Different Cultures?	56
2.4	Why Should a Start-Up Care about Culture?	60
2.5	Why Should a Growing Business Bother about Culture?	62
2.6	Why Should Culture Be An Important Consideration When Forming A JV or During An M&A?	64
2.7	Why Should Culture be an Important Criterion When Hiring New Talent?	68
2.8	Do Customers Care about Culture?	70
2.9	Do Investors Care About Corporate Culture?	72

2.10	Why Should We Try To Measure Culture?	74
2.11	Why Should an Organization's People System Be Aligned to Its Desired Culture?	76
2.12	Do We Have to Connect Every HR Initiative to Culture?	78

Exercise 2: Why Should You Assess Your Culture?   80

PART 3: HOW TO CREATE THE RIGHT CULTURE?   85

3.1	How Do I Know If the Time Is Right to Assess Our Culture?	86
3.2	How Important Is Culture Assessment When We Have so Many Other Priorities?	90
3.3	How Is Culture Assessment Done?	94
3.4	How Is a Culture Change Program Undertaken?	98
3.5	Will Culture Change Programs Deliver in Short-Term?	102
3.6	Why Do Culture Change Programs Often Fail?	104
3.7	What are the Practical HR Tools to Shape Culture?	108
3.8	As a Leader, How Can I Influence Culture?	112
3.9	As a Startup, How Do We Formally Define Our Culture?	114
3.10	How Does an Organization Cope with Cultural Challenges in its Midlife?	118
3.11	How Can We Approach Culture in Case of Joint Ventures or Mergers and Acquisitions?	122
3.12	How Does an Organization Handle Culture as it Expands to New Geographies?	124

3.13	Within a Big Organization, How Can We Set up a Winning Culture at the Team Level?	128
3.14	How to Get High Levels of Performance from Multi-Cultural Teams?	132
3.15	How Can We Build a High-Performance Culture?	136
3.16	How Can We Build a Culture of Adaptability in a Rapidly Changing Business Environment?	138
3.17	How Can We Create a Culture of Service Excellence?	142
3.18	How Can We Build a Culture Where Innovation Thrives?	146
3.19	How Can a Culture of Trust and Transparency Be Built to Raise Performance?	150
3.20	How Can We Create a Culture That Supports the Digital Transformation of Our Organization?	154

Exercise 3: Roadmap for a Cultural Change Program — 158

Summing It Up — 165
Acknowledgments — 167
About Ajit Mathur — 169

Preface

Leadership, strategy and culture are the three pillars on which organizations build success regardless of their size or business. While the first two have been extensively covered in articles and books, the third, culture, which is key to competitiveness, growth and performance seems to be ignored. In a typical business setting where numbers and matrices are given greater importance, culture is often considered not concrete enough to worry about.

This book is an attempt to demystify culture for practicing managers and leaders who would like a quick and precise understanding of an important element of organizational performance. For those who never had an opportunity or reason to think about culture, this book will serve as a valuable resource to help you get started.

Written in the form of a series of questions and answers, this book contains three main parts:

- **Part 1: What?** This section aims to help you gain an understanding of the foundational concepts of culture.
- **Part 2: Why?** This section focuses on why one should bother about culture in the first place.
- **Part 3: How?** Finally, the last section provides you with practical ideas to implement initiatives to assess, improve and cultivate culture.

Each part ends with a simple do-it-yourself exercise to help you reflect on your organization's culture in the context of its unique business challenges.

Written and designed as an easy and quick read for today's busy professionals, the book should not take more than 90–120 minutes to leave you with a gist of what culture is, why it matters and how you can improve it.

In the end, if you gain a clear understanding of culture, take away a few actionable ideas or develop a fresh perspective on your organization's culture, I would have succeeded in my endeavor.

Guys, so far we were told...
culture eats strategy for breakfast...
...nowadays, it also eats technology,
something we should be concerned about
Management 101
Ajit

PART 1

What Is Organizational Culture?

(But) Once you have acquired what I would call a "cultural perspective," you will be amazed at how rewarding it is. Suddenly, the world is much clearer. Anomalies are now explainable, conflicts are more understandable, resistance to change begins to look normal and most important, your own humility increases. In that humility, you will find wisdom.

**Edgar H. Schein,
Professor Emeritus, MIT Sloan School of Management**

1.1 What is Organizational Culture?

Imagine you are invited to witness meetings in two different organizations. In the first organization, you see employees, regardless of their position, challenging each other with ideas based on supporting data. In this place, the quest is for transparency and for the best idea to win. In the second place, however, you observe people generally keeping quiet and respecting the hierarchy. Here, the senior-most leader hands down a decision at the end of a gentle discussion and everyone agrees. This is organizational culture in action.

In essence, culture is a set of behaviors that are valued and followed in an organization. These behaviors are a result of people navigating challenges together, under the stewardship of the founder or a professional leader and in most situations is considered a valid formula for success. In practical terms, culture is reflected in how people think and act in different situations — how employees treat customers, how they collaborate, how they make decisions, how they handle diversity and so on. Culture also determines how an organization views and handles a variety of behavioral issues such as freedom, risk, innovation and short-term vs. long-term trade-offs.

Culture is like a magnetic field — an invisible force that shapes the behavior of a whole organization by shaping individual behavior. It is readily passed on to new members of the organization.

1.2 What Does Culture Look like if Dissected?

To get a good sense of an organization's culture, examine it at three different levels:

Top Layer: Artifacts

These are tangibles—easy to see and feel. For example, office décor, layout, uniforms and some visible behaviors—these form the top-layer of culture.

Example: In many offices, you see employees wearing formal dresses like company uniforms or suits, while in some others, you see people moving around in casuals. In both cases, you carry away an impression of their respective cultures, although they may not be able to explain their actual behavior by themselves.

Middle Layer: Espoused Values

Normally handed down by the founder of an organization, values are often reflected in annual reports, websites and office walls. But, by looking at the stated values, you can't be sure these are truly followed.

Example: If "excellence in customer service" is a value, employees of such an organization should be able to tell you, with pride, stories of how somebody went out of the way to help a customer. However, if no such stories exist, most likely, this value is only espoused but not followed.

Bottom Layer: Core Assumptions

At the bottom-most layer reside core assumptions, which are the founder's deep-seated assumptions that if "so and so" path is followed, the organization will be successful. As an organization

What Does Culture Look like if Dissected?

grows and new people join, they either reinforce or dilute these core assumptions. Almost everything that truly matters in the context of culture is a reflection of core assumptions.

Example: If a product launch was stopped mid-way due to minor glitches or a diversification bid was vigorously pursued in spite of perceived risks, only core assumptions can explain these behaviors.

Assimilating the "culture clues" from all the three layers—artifacts, espoused values and core assumptions—leads to the complete understanding of an organization's culture.

[Note: I am indebted to Edgar H. Schein, Professor Emeritus, MIT Sloan School of Management, for originally giving us this basic idea of viewing culture as a three-layer structure.]

1.3 | What Comes First—Strategy or Culture?

In most organizations, a strategy grabs leadership's attention first, as it offers a concrete and logical way to achieve the organizational objectives. The strategy often involves making a conscious choice among alternative products or service positions, customer segments, value propositions—a territory that everyone can relate to easily.

Culture, on the other hand, is invisible, qualitative and abstract. Being used to dealing with tangible subjects, leaders view cultural issues as "soft" and might end up placing it on a lower priority.

Even though in practice, leaders often focus on the strategy first, the two ideas—strategy and culture—are inextricably entwined. One without the other is incomplete. In fact, culture limits the strategic choices, e.g. a food company like Nestle would hesitate to invest in a strategy that takes it away from its core, however attractive it may be, because cultural underpinnings would silently argue "this is not who we are."

However, once a strategy is formulated and clearly articulated, it makes immense sense to check its alignment with the existing culture. When aligned with strategy, culture produces remarkable results, but when the two are not aligned it becomes a constraint, leading to sub-optimal results.

1.4 What Does an Enabling Culture Look Like?

Very often, as you step inside the premises of an organization and start dealing with it as a customer, a vendor, an investor or even as a job applicant, you get a flavor of their culture. The clues to their culture are all around and are often reflected in the behavior of the employees.

Prompt and constructive responses to customer queries, problem-solving attitude and empathetic behavior are the outward manifestations of an enabling culture. You are most likely to find energized and empowered employees, all aligned to a common mission. Such organizations are also likely to show strong market and financial performance.

On the other hand, organizations that do not enjoy enabling culture are characterized by sluggish work environment and an uninterested workforce drifting hopelessly or in the worst case, politicking. Their market standing and financial performance are likely to be uninspiring.

Lastly, pick a few employees from culturally rich organizations and you will find them filled with pride. They can easily narrate why they love their work and what kind of impact it is creating for the customers and society.

1.5 | Who Decides What Culture We Need?

Culture often starts with the founders of an organization. They start up with a passionate mission and a set of strong beliefs—the seeds from which culture sprouts over time.

If you could go back to Hewlett Packard of 1940s and sit with the founders Bill Hewlett and Dave Packard, you would find them talking passionately about how scientific instruments would change the world and their core belief that if talented engineers were provided an enabling environment to thrive around this mission, they would do remarkable things. You can almost predict what kind of employee behavior HP of earlier days would reward.

As the organization grows, founders fade away and companies induct professional CEOs. The Board starts exerting its influence and so do analysts, shareholders, customers, etc. In this phase, firms often find themselves at crossroads— should they continue to follow the original path that brought them success in the first place or chart out a new course? To recover the ground lost to Amazon, Apple and Google, Satya Nadella, Microsoft's new CEO, has been trying to orient Microsoft's culture in a new direction. He says, "We will grow as a company if everyone, individually, grows in their roles and their lives." Satya describes the new emerging culture based on this core belief as "growth mindset" because he believes a *dynamic learning culture* is needed to realize Microsoft's bold new ambitions and not a static model of culture that feeds off past success.

So, who decides the culture? Initially, the founders and later the professional CEO plays a pivotal role in shaping the culture.

1.6 Is It Beneficial to Involve All the Employees in Deciding the Values of an Organization?

When Sam Palmisano took over as the CEO of IBM in 2002, he did something unusual—he asked all 320,000 IBM employees, spread over 170 countries, to share their opinion on corporate values. Thousands of employees participated in what was dubbed as "Values.jam," an open forum on the company's Intranet, generating over 10,000 suggestions in a matter of 72 hours on the values IBM should follow.

Why would an organization attempt such a messy and gigantic exercise? Why can't the CEO and the leadership team decide the organizational values by themselves?

Sam realized that the values espoused by Watson, the founder, in 1914 had already lived for 90 years without being questioned, but for IBM's future, it was necessary to involve employees to create future values and hence the culture.

If we examine his process, first, he recognized that the original values did not support the strategy going forward (e.g. a value like "Pursuit of Excellence" became an excuse to avoid listening to customers, encouraging inward looking behavior). Next, he also sensed the challenge of galvanizing such a large workforce around new values and that it would be less formidable if the employees participated in shaping them.

After distilling the huge amount of data through focus groups and inputs from senior leadership comprising top 300 executives, the company came up with the new values or principles, as follows:

- Dedication to every client's success
- Innovation that matters—for the company and for the world
- Trust and personal responsibility in all relationships

Is It Beneficial to Involve All the Employees in Deciding the Values of an Organization?

As a result of the new values, IBM rejuvenated and its performance improved.

The lesson for leaders is simple—while the process could involve only the senior leadership group or a carefully chosen cross-section of employees or all the employees, the ultimate responsibility for culture still rests with the CEO. Not many organizations follow what IBM did, but it does demonstrate the value of participation as a tool in culture assessment and change.

If you wish to take this path of extensive participation, do remember that the outcome of this kind of exercise rests very much on whether your organization values transparency, debate and trust as prerequisites. Many modern day firms, especially technology ones, seem to follow this path.

1.7 What if We Don't Have a Written Document on Culture?

Many organizations don't see the need for defining culture in writing, but it is a very critical step. Defining cultural framework—mission and core values—in the form of a one-page document can provide the organization with a permanent reference to assess and help cultivate the desired culture. Of course, if the document is just to manage public perception, it is of no value, but if it truly reflects what the organization believes in, it is a great motivator for superior performance.

When the cultural framework is not defined in writing, the risk is that the organization may end up creating a culture—in default mode—that could be the result of whims and fancies of a few aggressive players or a haphazard collection of varied individual perceptions about the organization's values. Such a culture can't be a sustained high-performance, enabling one.

Consider Zappos, Amazon and Google. Their founders put in considerable effort in the early days to document their ideas on the values that these organizations cherished and continue to hammer these principles at every possible opportunity. Creating a culture is a deliberate act that all great companies always take very seriously.

A written document is also a great tool to attract as well as induct new team members, besides providing clarity to the entire organization.

If you don't have your cultural framework defined, just conduct a simple exercise: Ask a dozen people in your organization to describe your core values and mission. From the responses, you should be able to see how divergent their ideas are about your own culture in the absence of a written document.

1.8 Is There One "Right" Culture That Every Organization Should Aim to Imbibe?

No, there isn't. It is natural to be drawn to successful organizations and fall for the temptation to copy their culture. In every industry, a leader attracts the attention of all the other players and serves as a role model, but the strength of an organization lies in its uniqueness.

For example, all new tech companies would be tempted to copy the culture of Google, which is clearly explained in various places, including Google's own website. You can visit them and observe it in action. But it can't be easily replicated even if you know all the details about some other company's culture because the evolution of no two organizations can ever be identical. In fact, successful companies pay huge attention to defining and nurturing their own culture, for they know it is their permanent edge over competitors.

At the very core, even two competing and successful organizations may hold entirely different perspectives on culture, which brings uniqueness.

Instead of hoping to copy the "right" or "perfect" culture from somewhere else, it is far better to define and cultivate your own unique culture, based on your beliefs.

1.9 Is Culture a Constant Regardless of the Progress and Growth of an Organization?

No, culture is not a constant as its relevance depends on the context, which can change as the organization matures and grows.

Sometimes the very culture that makes an organization successful could become the reason for its decline. Successful organizations tend to become complacent and even arrogant, making it extremely difficult to change, even though the external environment demands a new cultural perspective. Almost all the cases of once highly successful firms like Kodak, Nokia, HMV share this characteristic. Some perish and others like IBM and Ford struggle for years to make the requisite changes in culture, paying a heavy price in terms of lost opportunities, growth, profitability, morale and talent loss. Microsoft is a good example of a company that has woken up to realize that it can't continue with the old culture and that it needs to be more agile, risk-taking and innovative to meet the current and future technological and business challenges.

The lesson is clear from both failed and successful companies: Culture is not static; it needs periodic review and refreshment to suit the emerging business challenges and context.

1.10 What Are the Key Ingredients of Culture?

To create its own unique culture, an organization needs the following four ingredients:

- Mission
- Core values
- Values or cultural attributes
- Actionable behavior

Mission and core values form the foundation of culture.

Mission answers a very basic question: Why are we doing what we are doing? Why does our business exist? Look at any successful organization and you will see a compelling mission galvanizing and driving its employees to fulfill some worthy cause. For example, Google is driven by the mission of "organizing the world's information and making it universally accessible and useful," a hugely challenging undertaking that has been propelling it to evermore greater heights.

Values, including core values, are principles or beliefs that the organization lives by. At Amazon, one of the core values is customer centricity, which means thinking on behalf of the customer, lowering prices, offering convenience and innovating. Everything that Amazon does must be consistent with this core value.

Besides core values, the other values commonly found across organizations include integrity, collaboration, transparency, sustainability, etc. These principles or ideals set a framework of behavior for employees to follow in the day-to-day conduct of business. Also called "cultural attributes," sometimes they are broken down further into specific, easy to comprehend, sub-attributes. For example, "risk-taking" may have several

What Are the Key Ingredients of Culture?

sub-attributes such as creativity, innovation, experimentation and tolerance to mistakes.

Further, each value or cultural sub-attribute when expressed in easy to understand and actionable language, is termed as an "actionable behavior."

1.11 What Is a Worthy Mission?

A worthy mission is authentic, clear and inspiring. It is simple and yet it is powerful. It is not just a set of carefully chosen words; according to Peter Drucker, a mission has to go beyond just good intentions; it must stimulate the right action.

Mission directs an organization's limited attention, resources and actions in a specific direction. It provides meaning and significance to employees in the day-to-day conduct of their jobs.

Sometimes, when organizations stray away from their mission, invariably the result is confusion and poor performance. Consider Starbucks whose original mission centered around an exceptional cup of coffee, handcrafted and served with passion, which helped build a new social space away from home and office. And then, somewhere along the company's success, the focus shifted to market growth, number of stores and the like, resulting in declining performance, prompting Howard Shultz, the founder, to come back and rescue his ship.

Paying attention to the mission is a great first step in building an organization's culture.

1.12 | What Do the Core Values and Values *Really* Represent? Are They Different?

Both the terms "core values" and "values" represent basic principles or beliefs around which an organization operates and many organizations use the terminology "core values" and "values" interchangeably. Organizations also use their own preferred expressions: Amazon calls them "leadership principles" and Netflix "core philosophy & real values." However, understanding them at a level deeper is useful.

The core value is a deeply held assumption about a strategic path an organization takes to be successful. For Apple, it is elevating user experience through excellence in product design. For Netflix, it is "people over process," signifying the freedom employees enjoy in delivering high expectations. For Amazon, it is "customer centricity." Usually, an organization operates based on one or two core values.

Besides the core value, an organization also believes in several other principles, typically four to five such as ethics, sustainability, social responsibility, fairness, etc. These are often called the "values." Some values like "ethics" draw a boundary that nobody should cross. Others like "caring for the environment" show a desirable direction. A value like "fairness" represents a principle which when applied to a variety of situations over time, tends to evolve in its meaning and application.

Highly successful organizations carefully articulate and nurture both their core values and other values as a reflection of the founder's full spectrum of beliefs. And that often distinguishes them from their competitors.

1.13 What Is the Role of Values in a Day-To-Day Job?

Values are what an organization stands for. In a practical sense, values guide the organization to structure, distribute roles and responsibilities, formulate HR policies and systems. Also, they guide the employees on how to conduct themselves and what behaviors to expect from others. In situations where either the organization or a team or an individual could choose from amongst multiple alternative paths, values help identify the path that best aligns with the organization's culture.

Suppose an organization is working on designing a new performance assessment system, should it open the project to a full-blown debate amongst employees or share some salient features with them to seek their feedback or just let employees know once the system is ready for a roll out? The choice will depend upon whether the organization believes in "openness," and whether "transparency" and "trust" are its values or not?

Another key characteristic of values is that if the actual behavior is not consistent with the *real* values, it generates resentment or an aggressive discussion and the people responsible are seen as "not behaving as expected." For instance, if transparency is a strongly held value and for some reason, adequate details are neither shared nor debated on a critical issue, one can expect a fair amount of disappointment and pushback from employees, which in turn is likely to lead to the right action.

Finally, values are routinely used in making important decisions, discussing new initiatives, getting work accomplished in teams, recruiting new team members (in some cases, separating team members), rewarding, etc.

Since values and in turn, culture reinforce group behavior, they help in bringing a degree of order and predictability to how an organization operates.

1.14 Do Values Evolve Over Time?

Yes, they do. Values are not static; they are living, breathing principles that evolve and guide individuals as well as organizational choices all the time.

Take a value like "meritocracy," which is the cornerstone of the culture of Bridgewater Associates, world's leading hedge fund. Ray Dalio, the founder, believed that working in an environment of transparency, highly talented people can produce spectacular results. Initially, it meant building a team that was comfortable having "thoughtful disagreements." As the company grew, Ray realized that he needed a system to bring transparency to all the employees and thus he decided to record all the meetings. This new level of transparency led to yet another insight—people have a unique way of thinking as a result of their personality and that it would be best if their personality profiles are openly shared. This will ensure allocating the *right* people for the task at hand, all aimed at producing the best result. As can be seen, meritocracy as a value or a principle kept evolving, both in meaning and scope, over time. New processes were added to reflect its changing scope.

Organizations that do not nurture values consciously may end up with espoused values that no longer mean anything substantial. It's best to revisit the values each time a difficult or a new situation confronts the organization and reflect on why a particular path was chosen. Is there some learning from the past? Is this situation any different? Is this decision going to define who we are and what we stand for? Does this principle or value need deeper reflection?

Vibrant organizations treat values as living entities that need to be looked after and nourished to build a healthy culture.

1.15 How to Convert Values into Actionable Behavior?

Values often sound like ideals and employees may not always relate to them in their day-to-day work. But culture is not about a set of words declared as values; it is all about routine behavior.

To turn values into real culture, values should be fleshed out in actionable language. This brings clarity and largely eliminates personal assumptions around broader concepts of culture or values.

For example, if *Open Communication* is a value of an organization, it could be turned into actionable behavior with a statement like below:

Share all the relevant information freely with your team members, which improves the quality of decisions or task execution. Similarly, encourage all your team members to express themselves or ask doubts without any fear of embarrassment. This will enable them to contribute more, build trust and raise your team's performance.

Also, ask yourself: Do I communicate enough to ensure that everyone concerned understand what I am trying to say? Do I give enough opportunity to other team members to freely express themselves?

By defining actionable behavior, employees get a strong signal to uphold values.

Each value of an organization should be described in the form of actionable behavior and this simple act moves values from the realm of theory and mere ideals into real practice and habit.

1.16 What Is the ROI on a Culture Change Program?

This is the favorite question of those who consider culture to be a "soft" issue with little connection to hard numbers. Indeed, it is very easy to shoot down any culture-related initiative, as it does not lend itself to the same quantitative analysis as, say, advertising's impact on sales. But that's where the pitfall for most organizations lies.

There are two answers to this ROI riddle. First, empirical evidence suggests that culture indeed impacts performance and in very significant ways. The real problem is how to isolate its impact and show returns when we know performance depends on some other factors as well. Second, either you believe in its power based on the experience of some of the world's leading organizations or ignore it at your peril.

Another way to view any investment—leadership time, effort, money—in a culture-related program is to evaluate its possible impact in the absence of it. If a business fails to meet its challenges and thus falls short of the desired performance outcomes, one should ask: What culture do we have? What if we can improve it to meet our business challenges? And what if we do nothing?

Investment in building an enabling culture is not a luxury; it is a need that the world's most successful companies like Apple, Google and 3M recognized long back. And they continue to invest in it to stay distinctive and enjoy the unassailable competitive advantage.

1.17 | Who Owns the Culture? Who Are the Key Stakeholders?

There are three primary stakeholders: The CEO, the Board and the top leadership team. And then come the remaining stakeholders—employees. But many organizations don't view culture with so many stakeholders.

Assuming that the Human Resources or People Operations department should take care of culture is a short-sighted approach. If there is a Chief Culture Officer, the temptation to leave everything to him or her may be even greater. But culture is far too important to be left to one particular department or an individual.

Among all stakeholders, CEO must take the responsibility to set the tone for the kind of culture the organization needs. He must consult his senior leadership team or even a larger group, but in the end, he must own it. The Board is also an important stakeholder to ensure that the CEO's cultural agenda is right for the organization and should play the role of providing wisdom and oversight on such a crucial issue.

After the CEO, senior leaders play an important role in shaping the culture as well in serving its custodians. They are the role models for the rest of the employees.

Finally, employees at large need to align their day-to-day behavior in line with the values the organization cherishes. With their routine behavior, they can either reinforce or weaken the culture of their organization.

In an organization that takes pride in its mission, values and culture, it is not uncommon to see everybody—from CEO down to the lowest rung employee— contributing to the culture in their own way.

1.18 What Is the Board's Role in Shaping Cultural Agenda?

In general, Boards do not pay as much attention to culture as needed and devote most of their attention to financial results, strategy, new business, compliance and compensation issues.

Even though the CEO is the primary custodian of culture, the Board should ask for periodic updates on culture. For example, the Board can discuss an assessment of a culture exercise or debate what culture the organization needs or identify culture-related challenges. If the CEO is also the Chairman of the Board, then his responsibility to put culture on the Board's radar is even more.

For an organization that treats its culture on par or even higher than strategy, the culture should be on the Board's regular agenda for discussion. The Board's views on culture should be sought particularly if a new strategy is being introduced or if there is a shift in the business environment needing a cultural alignment. The Board also needs to consider culture-related issues when a joint venture or a merger or an acquisition is under consideration.

Another situation where the Board should contribute on the cultural front is when a new CEO or any senior leader is being inducted. At the time of top leadership change, cultural foundations can suddenly become shaky.

Overall, Boards should play an active role in keeping an oversight on an organization's culture, making sure the mission and values are not diluted and that the CEO's cultural agenda is right for the organization.

Exercise 1: Your Organization's Culture—a Quick Assessment

With the following three steps, you can get a quick glimpse of the contours of your organization's culture.

Step 1: Select six cultural attributes

To keep things simple, let's select the following six attributes for your culture assessment:

1. Mission orientation
2. Customer centricity
3. Commitment to quality
4. Collaboration
5. Transparency
6. Innovation

Step 2: Rate your culture

Next, rate your organization's culture, based on what you observe in reality, on the six attributes selected in Step 2 in the table below:

1 = Strongly Disagree

2 = Disagree

3 = Neither Agree nor Disagree

4 = Agree

5 = Strongly Agree

Cultural Attribute	Description	Your Rating
Mission orientation	My organization has a well-defined and inspiring mission.	
Customer centricity	Customer service is our key value. In all our key decisions and actions, we keep the customer's viewpoint ahead of internal considerations.	
Commitment to quality	We are passionate about delivering outstanding quality of products and services.	
Collaboration	Cooperation with other team members in the same function and across other functions/ divisions/ locations is easy and comes naturally to achieve our goals.	
Transparency	Our organization encourages free flow of information, thus facilitating the best solution to any problem. It's easy to seek clarification on any aspect of organizational working, which allows building trust and promotes excellence.	
Innovation	The organization is very supportive of innovative thinking and encourages us to take intelligent risks without worrying about mistakes.	

Step 3: Draw the contours of your culture

Based on the ratings in Step 2, draw the contours (see Exhibit 1) of your organization's culture for an impactful visual representation of your current culture.

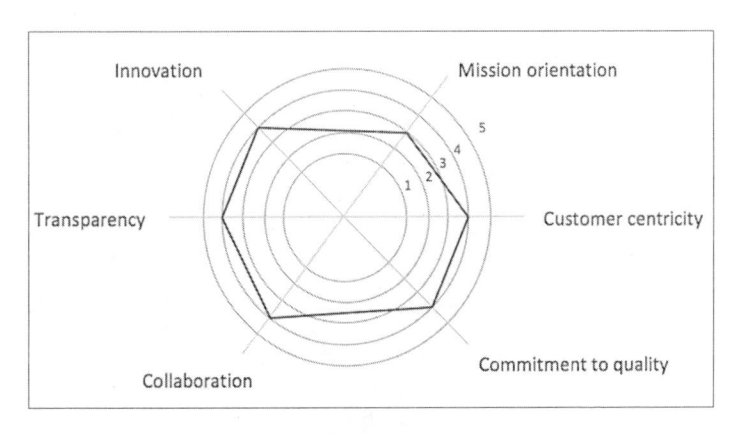

Exhibit 1

The above is just a sample for a quick assessment. In an actual culture assessment exercise, many more cultural attributes are rated. For your business, some may be more important than the others. When the results of an individual assessment are debated in a team setting, valuable insights into the present culture can be gained. Further, when such assessments are carefully complemented with qualitative assessment findings, culture can be understood with greater clarity.

Notes

PART 2

Why Does Organizational Culture Matter?

Building a culture (of high standards) is well worth the effort and there are many benefits. Naturally and most obviously, you are going to build better products and services for customers—this would be reason enough! Perhaps a little less obvious: people are drawn to high standards—they help with recruiting and retention... once you have tasted high standards, there is no going back.

**Jeff Bezos,
Founder & CEO, Amazon.com**

2.1 Why Does Culture Matter?

Many organizations wonder if culture is indeed a critical element to their success, but whether we make conscious attempts to shape culture or not, a default culture is in the making all the time. So, even if you choose to ignore the culture, it pretty much exists.

The link between the two is not readily visible, but culture is one of the crucial pillars that supports the performance of your organization. Downward or stagnant growth and profitability, shrinking market share, low employee morale—all such problems often stem from a dysfunctional culture. On the other hand, high performing organizations invariably have a well aligned, facilitating culture.

Extensive research shows that organizations lacking high-performance culture are unlikely to raise their business outcomes to the next level, often struggling to cope with business challenges instead of riding opportunities proactively. Employees need a vibrant, positive culture to contribute their best as individuals and as teams, and similarly, the organization needs a cultural rationale to navigate business challenges.

In the words of Edgar Schein, a leading authority on culture, "If you do not manage culture, it manages you. The only thing of real importance that leaders do is to create and manage culture."

The questions that every organization should be asking:
1. Is your existing culture helping your organization or hindering you?
2. Are you aware of the contours of your culture or does it remain hidden?
3. Are you aware of the impact of your culture on the organizational performance?

2.2 We Are Successful—Why Should We Care about Culture?

If your organization has done well, it means your culture has been conducive to your success and growth. But does it imply that the same mission, values and behavior that brought you up to this point are good enough for you to face the challenges in the future?

Consider IBM. If you were to step into the office of Tom Watson Jr. at IBM in, say 1960, you would be meeting a very proud CEO whose company's culture, popularly known as IBM Way, was the gold standard for success. But thirty years later, when Louis Gerstner arrived as the CEO of IBM, he was dismayed to see that IBM's culture no longer met the new demands of customers who were looking for solutions and services, and not pieces of hardware. The individualistic salesmanship, internal competition, proprietary standards must give way to cooperation, open standards and an approach to solve customers' problems, he concluded. Microsoft's story of success is similar. After achieving near monopoly in the operating system and office software, the company faltered and gave way to Google and Apple. Now Microsoft is in the process of reinventing itself by refreshing its mission and culture.

Examples like these and many other organizations underscore a key lesson: success leads to a strong culture which in turn, leads to complacency, and then when change is really required, the organization fails to respond. And eventually, the organization pays a huge penalty with key customers abandoning the ship, shareholders' wealth being wiped out and talented employees leaving the organization.

Successful organizations should review and reflect on their culture—mission, core values and behaviors—periodically, say, once a year and ask three key questions:

We Are Successful—Why Should We Care about Culture?

1. Is our current culture—actual behaviors—well aligned with our mission and values?
2. Is our current culture helping us deal with our immediate needs or are we stuck with problems that could be due to dysfunctional culture?
3. Is our culture suitable for new challenges we are likely to face in the future?

2.3 Can Different Parts of the Same Organization Have Different Cultures?

When organizations are young and small, a uniform culture throughout is highly desirable. But as they grow, it is not uncommon to find slightly different or sometimes very different sub-cultures amongst different functions or divisions of the same organization.

At a basic level, culture is a common set of values and behaviors associated with a group of people working together. So it is possible that one division, say, followed delegation and trust as key behaviors because the divisional head strongly believed in these ideas and was successful. In another division, a different divisional head believed in the idea of centralization and discipline, and his division was also successful. So who is right?

In a company like 3M, you may find R&D division enjoying the freedom to experiment with an added emphasis on individual accomplishment while the manufacturing division is operating with a greater focus on standardization, processes and productivity. What binds them however, is 3M's mission of "improving lives of people around the world with innovative products." In case of a large organization, it is important to assess whether these sub-cultures are serving the overall organizational mission or whether these are in conflict.

Sub-cultures could also be a natural response to external challenges. For example, a new initiative to strengthen design or technology can lead to increasing dominance of behavior associated with these functions. Similarly, internal challenges like growing complexity can lead to decentralization with each division or unit gaining some freedom to create its own sub-culture.

Can Different Parts of the Same Organization Have Different Cultures?

In case of a conglomerate, if different businesses are as diverse as airlines, IT services and chemicals, then it is actually advisable to give them the freedom to develop cultures relevant to their business or strategic context. But an overarching mission for the group as a whole should act as an overall guiding force.

2.4 Why Should a Start-Up Care about Culture?

All start-ups begin with a dream, an idea of a product or service and a supporting strategy, but highly successful ones set off with two more seemingly intangible ingredients: a mission and a set of core values as the foundation to their cultural journey.

Examining the early days of Google, Amazon and Facebook, it is clear that each one pursued their own unique value proposition to the customers, but as a company, they all centered around a clear mission and a set of values. As these organizations grew, their culture became a competitive advantage that others simply could not match. And they were even bold enough to document their cultural underpinnings and show the world as to what they stood for. Their distinctive culture became their brand. They advertised it, attracting talented people who felt inspired working in that culture. The investors knew what they were in for and customers loved doing business with these firms. As they became more and more successful, their culture became even more distinctive and stronger and in many ways, a source of unique identity.

Founders, thus, have this fantastic opportunity to lay the foundation of culture in the early days, which allows smoother scaling up. Start-ups also face several make or break challenges in the early days such as, deciding which products and partnerships to pursue or whom to hire; at every such juncture, culture distills the choices and guides the decisions meaningfully. Lack of a distinctive culture can result in inconsistent decisions.

So if you are a start-up, investing in forming a culture that aligns with your deeply held values can be an investment that would pay off multifold in the future.

2.5 Why Should a Growing Business Bother about Culture?

As organizations grow, new challenges appear in the form of new technologies, competitors and customer expectations. Almost in all cases, the culture that worked during the initial growth years no longer works against future challenges; in some cases, it takes as little as five to ten years to realize this or sometimes a bit longer.

The dilemma facing a growing organization is whether it should continue to pursue its original culture or take pains to examine and perhaps change parts of it to suit future challenges.

As a good practice, growing organizations shouldn't wait for a crisis—that would be a bit too late—but periodically review their culture and ask if the present momentum is likely to get threatened in any way should they stick to the present culture. In many cases, early signs of the problems can be detected through lead indicators such as customer churn or slippages in customer ratings, high employee turnover or high rework percentage. Forums like all-hands meeting or customer feedbacks or even market reports that provide critical analysis help corroborate these findings. Sometimes, talking to those who are directly in touch with customers, typically frontline employees, provides valuable clues to the strengths or weaknesses of the current culture. While not all performance issues could be a direct result of a dysfunctional culture, it's very crucial to evaluate the role culture could be playing.

Thus, growing organizations should always pay attention to their culture to ensure continued growth and success.

2.6 | Why Should Culture Be An Important Consideration When Forming A JV or During An M&A?

When two organizations decide to come together in the form of a joint venture, merger or acquisition, it is usually done with an assumption that synergies will be great, best talent will come together market share will grow. What is often forgotten is that the two entities coming together have their own cultures, which would invariably be different. The cultural disparity is one of the major reasons for failed joint ventures, mergers or acquisitions.

What is the solution? Ideally, even before you embark on such an exercise, assess the issue of cultural compatibility, giving it as much importance as other critical topics like product-market synergies or financial gains. Sometimes the result becomes highly uncertain because of cultural incompatibility itself.

If, however, the rationale for a JV or merger or an acquisition is so strong that it is assumed cultural integration issues would be taken care of post-deal, then a simple three-step process will help:

1. Top leaders of both the preceding entities must come together to discuss how the culture of the new entity would look like. Issues could range from understanding different missions, core values to possibly vastly different behaviors.
2. The CEO has to establish a common mission and core values, wherein both sides have to accept some changes to how they are used to working.

Why Should Culture Be An Important Consideration When Forming A JV or During An M&A?

3. Lastly, both sides need to understand that cultural integration takes time and some adjustments would have to be made through periodic reviews. Both sides have to give time and space for people to examine new behaviors and adjust to new reality.

In conclusion, if you are contemplating a joint venture, merger or an acquisition, cultural integration could hold the key to your future success.

2.7 Why Should Culture be an Important Criterion When Hiring New Talent?

Just like organizations, individuals also have values that are shaped by their background—country, city, education, family and friends. When hiring talent, you are essentially hiring a person with a unique set of values and if these values are largely in alignment with the organizational values, both sides will be better off. Conversely, misalignment can cause distress on both sides.

It is no surprise that leading organizations like Google, Netflix and Bridgewater Associates make enormous efforts to look for people who are likely to thrive in their cultures. The idea of culture-fit simply means hiring and retaining employees who are happy working in a particular culture.

By ensuring cultural fit, organizations spend less energy on inducting new talents who eventually become true brand ambassadors for the organization. When the cultural fit is poor, the employee in question is fighting against his own value system as well as the organization's culture, impacting his own physical and psychological health on one side and creating work-related issues on the other. For instance, Zappos, an Amazon company, offers not only remuneration but even a bonus to employees who wish to leave during the initial induction if they don't fit into the company's culture.

Organizations that exhibit sustained high performance spend a lot of time articulating what their culture means for prospective employees and then connect it to the hiring process.

2.8 Do Customers Care about Culture?

For some organizations, their mission and core values are synonymous with their brand. Apple epitomizes excellence in product design and Singapore Airlines excellence in service. Their products embody their core beliefs. Customers pay a premium because they care about these values. On the other hand, lack of a distinctive core value is a huge handicap for a brand.

But do customers *always* make buying decisions based on an organization's values? Although no proof exists to support this hypothesis, value- alignment does put customers in a favorable frame of mind towards a brand. Sometimes the values come shining through the brand as in the case of Apple and, sometimes, it's an indirect effect like in case of, say, a steel company that cares a lot about the local community and environment.

Some organizational values like openness or transparency or collaboration are very internal to an organization and may not make an impact on the immediate buying decision of a customer. But these are nonetheless correlated to the quality of service that the customer receives. In other words, culture spills out as customers interact with the organization.

To sum up, culture cannot be hidden from the customers. They care about culture to the extent that they see its impact on the final product or service. It is, therefore, a good strategy to align your brand's values with customers' values. If you can build your brand around your distinctive culture, you have taken a giant leap towards market dominance.

2.9 | Do Investors Care About Corporate Culture?

Yes, investors do care about culture because they understand that culture affects an organization's long-term economic performance.

Consider Howard Shultz, the founder and former CEO of Starbucks, who often animatedly talked about how Starbucks was investing in training baristas or how the company was offering its employees opportunities for further education or how the company was attracting new talent. From the investors' point of view, his words indicated determined efforts to create a unique culture that perfectly complemented their strategy.

Similarly, paying attention to Jeff Bezos, Amazon's founder and CEO, you'll know what's distinctive about Amazon's culture as he often passionately talks about how his team is super focused on customer centricity.

Still, how can investors know an organization's culture? Since there are no published results on culture unlike financial performance, there are two ways analysts and investors approach this subject. One, they assimilate facts from annual reports, analyst calls and business press. And second, they consult informed people in the business who know the intricacies. In the end, however, it's more of an art than science to decipher culture from indirect sources and factor in the quantitative analysis.

Investors do look for culture as it relates to the company's strategy and long-term future.

2.10 Why Should We Try To Measure Culture?

Can culture be measured? Expert opinions swing between yes and no. Some feel it's too complicated a construct and by measuring, we are essentially ignoring what's critical to form a culture but can't be measured: mission and core values. On the other hand, when we have no measurement in hand, we don't know what to improve or change and by how much. Without any measurement, it is also difficult to assess the progress of any culture transformation initiative.

So what's the way out? As a practicing manager, you can use a combination of qualitative and quantitative approaches. In the qualitative approach, try to identify the organization's mission and assess whether it's impacting people's behavior and key decisions. Also, devote time to unearth the core values—the assumptions that drive culture in a big way.

For the quantitative measurements, there are several well-known and validated methodologies to measure culture by conducting surveys and interviews. For example, it is possible to measure the culture of an organization along the dimensions of say, customer centricity, mission orientation, commitment to quality, collaboration, innovation and sustainability. Many others classify organizations along dimensions such as external vs. internal focus.

Think about it: having no measurement of culture versus having combined inputs from qualitative and quantitative approaches. Clearly, with an improved understanding of culture using a blend of both the approaches, you would gain a better grip, the power to shape your own culture and eventually the organizational performance.

2.11 Why Should an Organization's People System Be Aligned to Its Desired Culture?

In essence, culture is all about people and their behavior. These behaviors are shaped by what is valued, measured and rewarded in an organization. In fact, for any organization, its people or HR systems are the key levers for moving the culture in the desired direction.

Successful organizations continuously strive to align their systems and practices for recruitment, onboarding, performance management, rewards, succession, etc. with their culture. If, for example, one of the key cultural attributes is thinking out of the box and taking risks, then this quality will need to be identified during recruitment and encouraged through appropriate policies of performance management and rewards.

Without this kind of alignment, even if an organization decides on paper to have a certain kind of culture, its actual culture will diverge to undesirable directions. For example, almost all organizations want to promote the spirit of innovation, but how many have their HR systems aligned to encourage an atmosphere of free exchange of ideas and experimentation? One way out is reviewing each HR policy or process against the following criteria: Does it foster the values and behavior we cherish? Is it consistent with our core values? If the answer is somewhat unclear, it needs a review.

The CEO and senior leaders need to recognize that the people or HR systems need their support and attention, so that the desired culture is translated effectively into *working systems*. They also need to appreciate that such systems constantly evolve and are never perfect. The key is to periodically examine whether these are aligned with the desired culture.

2.12 | Do We Have to Connect Every HR Initiative to Culture?

One organization believes that reorganizing customer-facing teams is the way forward to meet the competitive threat and thus undertakes an extensive program. The underlying assumption is that once the initiative is implemented, culture will anyway change to reflect the greater agility it needs. Another one believes that agility as a value needs to be brought into focus to combat future business challenges and as a result, decides to undertake a program to reorganize customer-facing teams. Which approach is right?

Organizations can be found using both the approaches. However, the second approach has three distinct advantages. First, a higher level principle (value) brings clarity as to why a certain initiative is being undertaken and in moments of uncertainty and reflection, one can always claw back to that higher level principle. Second, it allows us to think if there is any other principle or value at play which needs emphasis (e.g. if becoming digital is an important value, then without emphasis on continuous learning, it is unlikely to yield the desired outcome). And third, it allows senior leaders to commit the threshold level of attention and resources for such an initiative to succeed.

Thus it is a good practice that when thinking about any HR initiative or change in a process or policy, first think of your cultural framework and arrive at sound reasoning as to which values are at play and why? It will help you arrive at a more robust framework to implement any new initiative.

Exercise 2: Why should you assess your culture?

This exercise will help you think through the need for culture assessment.

Step 1: External challenges

Describe the top three external challenges facing your organization which can severely affect the performance and competitiveness of your organization.

Example: Our pipeline of orders is drying up. New competitors seem to have better technology and offer better prices. How long can we rely on old products? We have many products that don't seem to fit customers' changing needs.

1. _____

2. _____

3. _____

Step 2: Internal challenges

Now, turn your attention to internal challenges. These are dysfunctional aspects of culture that might have taken root over time, and if not changed, can harm your business.

Example: We have far too much bureaucracy. There are so many hurdles in making simple decisions. It leads to poor response time and customers get restless. People have figured out their own ingenious methods to circumvent this maze. We lack transparency and freedom to express our opinions freely.

1. _____

2. _____

3. _____

Step 3: Desired values and behaviors

Lastly, think of values or behaviors that you think are necessary to navigate the future and are currently either missing or not considered important. Describe three such behaviors.

Example: We know innovation is important, but it is only discussed in meetings with no action on the ground. People are neither encouraged nor rewarded. If something goes wrong, they could even lose their job.

1. _____

   _____

2. _____

   _____

3. _____

   _____

Step 4: Making overall sense

By going through the three steps above, you would have a fair idea of whether the culture is fully working to your advantage or if it needs review. Many times, the present culture's dysfunctional aspects remain hidden as long as certain levels of performance goals are met. The problem usually begins when performance starts slipping and there is no straightforward remedy in sight, or when there is a tendency to explain variances based on external factors (changing market conditions, economy, etc.) instead of own culture-related issues.

A systematic review of present culture is the first step towards cultivating the desired culture, a culture that enables an organization to navigate the challenges and perform at its best.

Notes

PART 3

HOW TO CREATE THE RIGHT CULTURE?

The CEO is the curator of an organization's culture. Anything is possible for a company when its culture is about listening, learning and harnessing individual passions and talents to the company's mission. Creating that kind of culture is my chief job as CEO.

Satya Nadella,
CEO, Microsoft

3.1 How Do I Know If the Time Is Right to Assess Our Culture?

Typically, organizations do not worry about culture unless they face a crisis, which is the story of IBM, General Motors, Ford and Microsoft.

The culture-related crisis can manifest in different ways. One of the most obvious symptoms is continuous slippages in financial performance and market share in spite of all the good intentions and effort. British Airways was hit with such a problem in the early 1990s until Sir Colin Marshall arrived as the CEO in 1993 and made "excellence in customer service" as the centerpiece of his turnaround effort.

Sometimes technology or customers' expectations shift so rapidly that an internally focused organization is unable to respond, as in the case of Nokia. The former phone giant just couldn't come to terms with Apple's superior touch technology, features and design, operating in denial mode for dangerously long.

At times, the top management itself might sense that the organization is just too slow to respond to new opportunities like how Microsoft discovered after missing out on the early wave in mobile phones and then lagging behind in cloud enterprise business, playing catch up.

If your organization is facing any of the symptoms like falling profits, sliding market share, shrinking customer loyalty, inability to exploit emerging opportunities in spite of good intentions or a general climate of pessimism towards the future, it is time you looked at your culture with a heightened sense of urgency.

How Do I Know If the Time Is Right to Assess Our Culture?

The ideal approach is to build a formal mechanism to reflect on culture, say, every six months or at least yearly and ask: Is the current culture helping us move into the future with confidence? Is it aligned with the strategy? What has changed in our environment (technology, new competitors, demographics, etc.) that may require tweaking our culture?

3.2 How Important Is Culture Assessment When We Have so Many Other Priorities?

The question "Is cultural assessment a priority?" should be assessed in the context of three possibilities—ongoing crisis, future crisis and no crisis.

Crisis provides a tailor-made opportunity to bring in a change in culture. If you are already facing a performance crisis, culture should be near the top of your agenda. In practice, however, an organization facing crisis also has to tackle a whole bunch of other burning priorities such as revamping product line, refocusing on select segments, paring down expenses and improving services. While it's challenging for the leadership, in a crisis, cultural assessment should not wait. By conducting a quick assessment, the organization is always in a better position to respond to the ongoing crisis.

The second possibility is that an organization is enjoying a fair amount of success but its lead indicators are flashing warning signs. For instance, a competitor is slowly snatching away valuable customers with superior offerings or regulatory environment is changing or steady loss of talent. Should culture enter into the equation or just address the most visible problem directly? It's a tricky question, but if a small dent is likely to erode chunks of business or if a seemingly small problem could soon become a big problem, culture is once again worth looking at.

The third possibility is that a business is coasting along comfortably and there are no burning issues. There is a view that if you can't identify a compelling pain point, don't meddle with culture. But if you ask CEOs, they would straightaway tell you three or four major challenges facing the organization. By assessing its culture when things are going well, the organization enjoys the option to identify areas of emerging weaknesses and

How Important Is Culture Assessment When We Have so Many Other Priorities?

strengthen the same before it starts affecting organizational performance in a tangible way.

Ideally, say, an annual exercise to deeply reflect on culture is the best way to keep track of how an organization is operating in alignment with its mission and values and thus ensure continued success.

3.3 How Is Culture Assessment Done?

An organization culture assessment exercise is to establish a clear understanding of the present culture in the context of business challenges that the organization faces. Broadly, an exercise in culture assessment includes the following steps:

Constitute a Team

Culture assessment is a team effort. Led by the CEO, the team should include all senior leaders representing the key functions, divisions and geographies.

Lay Out the Business Challenges

Why the culture assessment? What's the rationale for the whole organization to spend effort, time and cost for the assessment? And so, set the context for culture assessment by identifying key business challenges. These challenges could be declining financial performance, erosion of market share, new competitors, new technology, desire to capture new opportunities or strengthening innovation. As you discover your mission, core values and behaviors in the subsequent steps, see which one is at a play about business challenges on hand.

Focus on the Mission

Mission provides *continuing inspiration* to an organization and its leaders. It helps clear the mist often formed by business challenges, which keep varying. Microsoft's CEO, Satya Nadella, for instance, has been leading the effort to discover Microsoft's soul or mission and then reorient its culture to counter and conquer the emerging business challenges.

How Is Culture Assessment Done?

Distill Core Values

Organizations run by certain core principles—assumptions about what will make them successful—and in practice, use these principles to take major decisions, e.g. choosing one product over the other or adding a particular key member to the team. In many cases, founders articulate these principles or core values. In other cases, the history of the organization provides important clues. In either case, by understanding the rationale behind key choices, we start understanding the organization's core values.

These core principles or values also include some implicit ideals such as integrity or transparency that the founder would have been passionate about. The key to understanding culture is to understand these values, not superficially but those *really at work*.

Supplement with Quantitative Assessment

In order to supplement the qualitative insights, there are several quantitative culture assessment tools available. Most measure employees' responses to a battery of questions through a survey. They measure behavior directly such as the extent to which collaboration is really a value or if openness is actually a highly valued behavior, etc. Results can often be sliced easily by levels, locations, etc. to get a greater insight.

Summing Up

A deep understanding of mission, core values and behavior in the context of business challenges provides an invaluable insight into the present culture.

3.4 How Is a Culture Change Program Undertaken?

Culture change or cultural transformation means shifting the present culture to a desired future culture. Here are the broad steps:

Establish a Clear Rationale for Change

As a starting point, an organization needs to link its cultural change program to business needs by identifying business challenges.

A traditional car manufacturer could frame culture change in the context of the threat posed by electric cars. For an offline retail company, e-commerce poses a big threat. Sometimes, an opportunity could trigger the culture change like it happened for GE when the company in early 2000 proactively decided to focus on digital and sensor technologies. In all cases, keep digging deeper till you can link problems or opportunities to cultural issues clearly.

Craft the Message for Change

Often a sense of urgency and compulsion—"if we don't change" message—is needed to drive the change. For example, Jeffrey Immelt, former CEO, GE, in 2001, proclaimed an "existential crisis" unless GE changed its strategic focus and culture. Culture change needs a compelling vision of how change will lead to an attractive future as also a scenario of how the future would look in the absence of any change.

Assess the Gap Between the Present Culture and Desired Culture

Present culture should be assessed through a formal assessment process. The desired culture, on the other hand, is a direct outcome of the question "what values and behavior do we need? How should we function in order to meet the future business challenges?"

The picture is complete when the desired culture is compared to inadequacies in the present culture. For example, lack of transparency and autonomy might be slowing down decision-making whereas the business needs quick decisions. These gaps between the present culture and desired culture then form the agenda for "what to change?" and "why?"

Design Interventions and Track Results

To change behavior, we need to change a policy, a process or the way work is organized or a combination of these elements. For example, if a culture of accountability is required, then redesigning the goal setting and performance feedback processes might be the key.

As culture change gets underway, periodically track key leading indicators as well as the results. It builds confidence and the possibility of timely course correction if required.

Demonstrate Resolve to Make New Behaviors Stick

Top leadership needs to demonstrate *through actions* that they are serious about change. They do it through their refreshed priorities, allocation of time, attention and other resources and the way they make decisions. Sharing regularly with employees as to why a certain path is being chosen and emphasizing through day-to-day examples is a great way of building a deeper appreciation of change.

The key to success in a culture change program is thus a clear and compelling vision, CEO's unwavering commitment, systematic approach, perseverance and demonstration through actions.

3.5 Will Culture Change Programs Deliver in Short-Term?

It's a mistake to expect short-term payoffs, say, on a monthly or quarterly basis, from a culture change program. The typical time horizon is 3–5 years or even more for large organizations. Scandinavian Airlines (SAS) took four years, Xerox seven years and GE something like 10 years to realize substantial dividends from their change programs. Says Chip Bergh, CEO, Nike, after successfully combating a decade of stagnating revenues, "I've also learned that it's very hard to change a culture... but now that we're growing again, the culture has been slow to change."

The Board, the CEO and other stakeholders should take a long-term view of a culture change program, knowing well that business outcomes like sales or profitability or customer ratings will follow once change starts taking root. At the same time, tracking leading indicators to assess whether a culture transformation initiative is moving in the desired direction is a good practice. For example, if an organization is reinforcing a value like "collaboration" in its culture change program, then it is helpful to measure it periodically through a well-designed employee survey.

Cultures are formed over a long period of time and it is natural that it takes time to change a culture. Question is whether the leadership has the conviction that cultivating the right culture would really make a difference to the organization's future success and then persevering through the journey of culture change.

3.6 Why Do Culture Change Programs Often Fail?

Almost 75% of the change programs do not deliver the intended results. Culture change is no different.

Successful culture transformation requires deep commitment, time, efforts and money. If an organization embarks on this journey without adequate preparation and a deep conviction, the change program is unlikely to produce the desired results.

First, the CEO and the top leadership team should debate, reflect and convince themselves of two critical elements: What needs to change and why? These basic questions set the trajectory of the whole transformation program. Choosing the wrong direction in a hurry without proper assessments of the existing culture and business challenges can be disastrous. Once the direction is decided, the leadership team should work diligently to put forward compelling arguments to buy the employees' commitment to the whole effort. Many organizations falter at this step itself, paving way for the eventual failure of the change program.

Next, it is critical to recognize that culture change is not about displaying new values or mission on walls, but about behavioral change, which is where the initiative often hits the wall of resistance. Any kind of change creates anxiety among people who perceive it as a potential threat to their position or remuneration or growth or the job itself. One solution is to create learning opportunities to practice new behavior and allow employees to experience what change could mean. For example, if the new system involves team-based rewards, then allow employees to discuss and visualize how that would work. Or pick an actual situation and take them through how it would be handled in the future. In short, provide training,

Why Do Culture Change Programs Often Fail?

coaching, feedback and counseling rather than forcing the change program at a pace that employees cannot handle.

It is also important to reshape the HR policies and systems such as performance management or rewards, to reflect consistency with the new expected behavior. Failure to do so can confuse and block the progress.

Finally, culture change inherently is a long journey involving surprises along the way. The leaders should be prepared to dig in for the long haul and make course correction along the way if necessary.

The awareness that culture change programs may not yield desired results without the full involvement of the top leadership is the best way to improve the prospects of success.

3.7 What are the Practical HR Tools to Shape Culture?

Organization structure, roles and responsibilities, recruitment, onboarding, recognition, performance management and communication process, all help shape a company's culture.

Structure, Policies & Processes

Organizational structure, designations, job descriptions, policies for compensation and leave, processes (say, an expense approval process)—all these HR elements can be used to reflect and strengthen a certain culture.

For example, should employees be trusted always to do the right thing or do they need close supervision and elaborate tracking systems? Depending upon the answer, you will accordingly design the structure, policies and processes which will either reflect a culture of freedom and trust or a culture of control and disempowerment.

Recruitment

While recruiting, most organizations focus on competencies and skills, but increasingly culturally-sensitive organizations are also assessing "culture fitness," which is an unassailable competitive advantage. For example, if your culture emphasizes diversity, including this factor in the selection process, is likely to bring in talent who would thrive in a diversified environment—and further reinforce the culture of diversity.

Onboarding

Inducting new employees into an organization's culture is as important as selecting the right candidates. Onboarding

What are the Practical HR Tools to Shape Culture?

programs provide a unique opportunity to build desirable behavior early on and that too in a relatively relaxed atmosphere.

Recognition

Public recognition of employees who live up to the organization's most cherished values is an important tool to build the right culture. For instance, if there is a system to recognize innovative ideas, it reinforces the culture of innovation. 3M, one of the most innovative companies, has infused innovation in its culture by placing high importance on rewarding innovative ideas and exhibiting a high tolerance for failures.

Performance Management

When performance management system is used as a tool to improve performance, the focus on behaviors such as collaboration or accountability yields rich dividends. Emphasizing on a specific behavior ensures that the desired cultural values are upheld and strengthened.

Leadership's Communication

Top leadership plays a pivotal role in clarifying and reinforcing key beliefs through regular communication. Following a process, there should be predictability to the frequency of communication (e.g. monthly All-hands Forum) and extent of engagement on culture-related issues—all critical to cultivating the desired culture.

All organizations operate with an array of HR tools. The key question is whether these tools are aligned with the desired culture?

3.8 | As a Leader, How Can I Influence Culture?

If you are the CEO or a senior leader, you are at the wheels, driving your organization's culture. As the CEO, you are the custodian of the culture—creating, preserving, or evolving it. If anything substantial has to improve or change in the culture of your organization, you have to take the lead. In other words, strategic culture related decisions are too important to be delegated downwards.

Specifically, you can influence the culture by articulating key beliefs and role modeling behaviors you desire to see around you. For example, your culture-related behavior is visible to others when you ask questions in meetings, make decisions, appreciate or criticize certain things and how you spend your time. Your behavior is likely to be mirrored across the organization.

If you talk about innovation but reprimand people on their mistakes, that straightaway dilutes your efforts to create an innovative organization. If you want customers to be treated fairly but allow sticking to policies that are not fair to your own employees, that again affects your culture of fairness. If you want to promote cost consciousness, but splurge on your own, employees get confused signals. In essence, leaders' behavior and decisions must be consistent with the desired culture.

No one else has as much leverage on culture as you have.

3.9 As a Startup, How Do We Formally Define Our Culture?

If you are the founder and have decided to formally define your culture in writing, this could be a pivotal decision in the journey of your organization. Today's giants like Google, Amazon, Starbucks and many others stand on the firm foundations of a well-defined culture.

Here are a few simple but powerful actions to lead a culturally-driven organization:

State Your Mission

Define your mission. Every founder has a dream, which at a deeper level, solves a problem or improves the well-being of a set of people in society. Reflect on it and put it in words. Then brainstorm with your colleagues and distill it down to a precise, inspiring statement. This is your mission–culture's North Star and one statement that can inspire and guide you and your employees for years to come.

Discover Your Core Values

What are your core values? Consciously or unconsciously, you use certain principles to run your organization. To bring these to the forefront, reflect on some of the key decisions you have made as a founder. Why did you make those choices? This kind of analysis will lead you to core values, a set of principles that drive your organization.

Arrive at Your First Working Document on Culture

Mission and core values define your cultural framework. Put them in writing in the form of "cultural manifesto" and discuss it with your Board. Refine it in future if necessary.

As a Startup, How Do We Formally Define Our Culture?

Craft Your Final Culture Manifesto

Next, share the cultural framework with all the employees and allow them to ask questions or give feedback. Refine the manifesto further if required and settle down on its final version.

Finally, start tracking your culture through periodic yearly reviews. As the organization faces newer challenges, see how your core principles play out; refine, if necessary.

3.10 How Does an Organization Cope with Cultural Challenges in its Midlife?

An organization arrives at midlife when the founder no longer holds command over key organizational decisions and instead, a professional CEO and the Board exercise much authority. At this stage, usually, the future business challenges look vastly different from what the organization is used to handling in the past. Making any change to culture is harder at this midlife stage because the assumptions that drive its culture are well entrenched.

The key is to skillfully change those elements of culture that are dysfunctional while retaining others. For instance, in the case of Microsoft, Satya Nadella, the CEO, has displayed remarkable maturity to connect with the founder's mission, while also embarking on a journey to change key elements of the company's culture such as encouraging a learning attitude and a new degree of openness. Thus one key lesson is that as the CEO, one should spend sufficient time on culture early on to achieve clarity on the unique identity of the organization—for self, employees and rest of the ecosystem.

The best way to systematically handle this challenge is to go through a formal culture assessment that enables the leadership to gain insights into its present culture. This is even more relevant if the organization is contemplating major changes in product lines, new technology, expansion, joint venture, acquisition, etc. as such initiatives place very different and new demands on culture. Adding to these challenges in midlife is often the impact of growth—more products, more geographies, more people – on culture the organization no longer resembles in its early years.

How Does an Organization Cope with Cultural Challenges in its Midlife?

The CEO plays a crucial role at this juncture, reasoning out his own position on culture in the light of the future strategy, specifically, what to retain and what needs change?

Thus an organization's mid-life cultural challenge hinges around skillfully managing cultural change to meet future business requirements.

3.11 How Can We Approach Culture in Case of Joint Ventures or Mergers and Acquisitions?

Joint ventures, mergers and acquisitions are usually formed around a business having complementary products, markets or technologies. Culture is generally ignored, assuming that *somehow* people from both the organizations will figure out how to work together. Usually, such mergers end with cultural clash because each organization brings with it the heavy baggage of its own unique culture.

Should the two organizations sort out the cultural issues even before they come together? Ideally, as the deal progresses, the two sides should also discuss the future culture of the new entity. And if some gross incompatibilities are detected, a joint strategy for forging a new culture should be drawn up including a periodic review mechanism.

At times, however, the approach could be to allow the new entity to function as if nothing has happened, like Microsoft's handling of LinkedIn, simply because cultural integration might be too complex and not even desirable.

Finally, an extremely effective communication program is required to appraise employees at all levels of the key components of the new culture—mission, values and specific behaviors. And they should be given an opportunity to ask questions and seek clarifications.

While tangibles like market share and financial data take center stage during joint ventures, mergers and acquisitions, culture remains in the background. But that's where lies either the risk of future fallout or an opportunity to script success.

3.12 How Does an Organization Handle Culture as it Expands to New Geographies?

As an organization expands into new geographies away from its home base, one of the dilemmas leaders face is whether its culture in the new territories should resemble the one at home or should it adapt to the local country or city culture?

The answer lies in appreciating the concept of "nested cultures," which means the culture of every organization exists within a larger societal culture, shaped by the country-culture and in many cases, a city or regional culture. These three levels of culture—organization, city or region and the country are nestled in one-another and they influence each other.

So how should an organization on the move to expand, handle its culture in a new location? At an elementary level, its mission and core values which bind the whole organization should remain the same irrespective of where its business units or operations are located. People take great pride in this common identity. It also serves to attract high-quality talent and builds a strong corporate brand.

Next, corporate leadership has to accept that each location has to deal with its own local needs and culture, and thus allow some flexibility in developing its own strategically relevant local culture. For example, in cultures where hierarchy matters more than the strength of an individual's ideas, attempts to encourage open debates are likely to yield chaotic results. Similarly, building consensus is a well-accepted behavior in some cultures and expecting people to quickly abandon it in favor of a faster, business-like approach may not be the ideal way. In all cases, the guiding principle should be whether the change required materially impacts business outcomes or not and move accordingly.

How Does an Organization Handle Culture as it Expands to New Geographies?

Finally, measured doses of rotation amongst the headquarter executives and local executives is a well-accepted solution to integrate various locational sub-cultures, allowing both sides to appreciate commonality as well as the need for local adaptation—all leading to the strengthening of the overall organizational culture.

Thus the key to managing culture in new geographies is to appreciate that culture comprises of unchangeable and flexible parts. Leadership should be clear about these two elements and carefully tweak the flexible elements to enable them to be well-nested in the local country or region or city culture.

3.13 Within a Big Organization, How Can We Set up a Winning Culture at the Team Level?

If you are leading a team, irrespective of its size and who the members are, you can not only influence the "local culture"—how team members accomplish a given task– within your team but also leverage it to achieve higher levels of performance. To shape the culture at the team level, start with the following:

Meaningful Work

At the very core, if you can connect your team members with the impact of their work, they would be inspired to achieve high levels of performance. When a team is exposed to even a small impact of its work, say, customer delight due to hassle free check-in and check-out at a hotel, it acts as a trigger for all members to come together and work harder.

Psychological Safety

If team members can air their views freely and frankly, without the fear of insecurity or embarrassment, it raises both the quality of discussions and decisions. Teams operating with higher levels of psychological safety enjoy greater levels of interpersonal trust, which translates into higher performance.

Collective Intelligence

The collective intelligence of a team, distinct from individual intelligence, allows it to perform well across a wide range of tasks. Collective intelligence rises when the leader promotes a behavior where each team member enjoys equal opportunity to express. This culture is opposite to a stifling environment where a few members dominate while forcing others into passivity.

Within a Big Organization, How Can We Set up a Winning Culture at the Team Level?

When members of a team can attach meaning to their work, enjoy psychological safety and operate at a higher level of collective intelligence, they create a team culture that can take their team to higher levels of performance.

3.14 How to Get High Levels of Performance from Multi-Cultural Teams?

With people from different nationalities and background working together in most organizations, multicultural teams are a common reality. Further, many team members may be remotely connected and the teams themselves may be changing to accomplish a variety of different tasks. Enabling such teams to perform at their best is one of the major challenges, which if not handled properly, can impact key values (e.g. a belief that bringing together diverse talent is a great way to enhance performance) and in turn, performance.

There are four ways such teams can raise their performance:

Bring Mission and Common Objectives to the Fore

A worthy mission often provides the glue to bind people from diverse backgrounds. A team leader should not only orient everyone toward the mission but should also provide the second layer of binding: team's overarching objectives (e.g. "we are here to solve X, which will help our firm in its mission Y").

Nudge them to Suspend Judgments about Each-others' Cultures or Mental Stereotypes

The first meeting (even within virtual teams) is always very important to establish trust and suspend personal judgments about each other. One proven way is to allow team members to "thaw" by letting them share their own stories or personal experiences or perceptions of the task at hand. This often brings a realization that people are really the same irrespective of their cultures.

How to Get High Levels of Performance from Multi-Cultural Teams?

Focus on the Task at Hand, not People

As the group digs in, the team leader should focus more on the task at hand than on individuals, thus showing how the output of the group as a whole is more important than individual brilliance.

Reward Group as a Whole

When the team members know that the reward or recognition of doing a good job will largely be attributed to the group as a whole, the behavior and underlying team culture are very different from a situation where individual performances overshadow group performance.

To achieve high performance, multi-cultural teams can follow a systematic process by coming together around a common mission, focusing on common goals and tweaking the reward system to emphasize team performance.

3.15 How Can We Build a High-Performance Culture?

The culture of high performing organizations has few things in common: strong leadership, focus on customers, willingness to experiment and humility in the face of a changing environment. In contrast, low performing organizations are characterized by lack of leadership, inward focus, resistance to change and arrogant attitude.

To build a culture of high performance, first, an organization needs strong leadership at the top. The cases of British Airways, General Electric, Xerox and many other firms illustrate that a strong leader who is willing to take the risk can trigger a change towards a culture of superior performance. Jack Welch at GE, for instance, orchestrated some dramatic changes in the way business was organized and operated. Contrast this with a leadership that sticks to the status quo while even ignoring hard evidence. Think about how Xerox's management ignored a great opportunity to bring personal computer to the market they invented in the early 1970s.

Secondly, the focus on customers is the hallmark of a high-performance culture. As customers demand superior products and services and competitors start chipping off market share, focus on customers becomes even more important. Consider the critical question that a giant like Walmart faces today: How should we respond to the threat of online retail? In a high-performance culture, issues like this trigger quick and decisive response.

Lastly, organizations that pay attention to employees' welfare and needs perform at a different level compared to those who don't care. Attracting and retaining talent is an important pre-condition to high-performance culture, which is often the gap between average and top performing organizations.

High-performance culture stands on three main pillars: strong leadership, customer obsession and talent.

3.16 How Can We Build a Culture of Adaptability in a Rapidly Changing Business Environment?

An adaptive culture—a culture that allows an organization to constantly adapt to the changing business needs—is a necessity in the face of highly uncertain and volatile business environment, e.g. constant disruptions caused by digital technologies. At the heart of it, people operating in an adaptive culture are enthusiastic to solve problems as they encounter and act on opportunities as they arise. Also, it includes an element of gazing into the future, anticipating what might come.

There are four key characteristics of an adaptive culture. One, it recognizes that strategy can change rapidly as the business environment shifts and hence does not resist change and new behavior. Second, it allows experimentation and has a large tolerance for mistakes. Third, it promotes transparency, openness and trust, which means employees enjoy a sense of ownership and need relatively less persuasion to change or act. Fourth, speed is valued over perfection.

In essence, adaptability is leadership and employee mindset that change is a way of life (than a once-a-lifetime event) and any conducive behavior is welcome. By embracing it as a formal principle or value, organizations can move the essence of this idea from "good to have" to "this is how we work."

To move towards an adaptive culture, the top leadership must demonstrate a *change in approach* to show what adaptation is all about. For instance, Microsoft's quick and decisive investment in "cloud" demonstrated its willingness to adapt. Similarly, its strong intent to play a role in quantum computing is an important signal that the organization is ready to experiment and place big bets for the future. Getting into an adaptive mode, Toyota is also responding to emerging challenges posed by

How Can We Build a Culture of Adaptability in a Rapidly Changing Business Environment?

digital, mobility and autonomous technologies by establishing a new organization, roles and partnerships; these changes will test its agility as well, given that the speed of change is critical to its future.

Almost all organizations need an element of adaptation in their culture. The only difference could be in the extent of emphasis and intensity of this value, as it relates to their specific challenges.

3.17 | How Can We Create a Culture of Service Excellence?

The leaders in service excellence companies like Singapore Airlines, Ritz Carlton, FedEx and Amazon have systematically built their culture by choosing extraordinary customer service as their key differentiator.

Services are mostly about people and their behavior, and the following three values are central to the culture of organizations pursuing service excellence:

Customer Centricity

If an organization can truly consider customers' viewpoint as paramount in its day-to-day work and all the important decisions, it takes a huge stride towards customer centricity. For instance, a simple decision like a small change in customer service procedure could be evaluated differently by different organizations depending upon the importance they attach to the value of "customer centricity."

Jeff Bezos, founder & CEO, Amazon has taken customer centricity to a whole new level, which he calls "customer obsession," which implies thinking, acting and even innovating on behalf of the customer.

Commitment to Quality

Organizations pursuing service excellence genuinely believe in delivering superior quality of products and services, and pay great attention to details. In these organizations, employees at all levels commit to this ideal and exhibit this behavior by not only fulfilling customers' expectations but strive to go beyond, looking for opportunities to delight customers.

How Can We Create a Culture of Service Excellence?

Respect for Individuals

Organizations with a culture of service excellence deeply care about their employees and basic human values. There is strong empirical evidence that such values translate into outstanding customer service. Employee care and respect include fairness, opportunity to grow and succeed, respecting diversity and the effort to accommodate individual aspirations.

The journey towards service excellence starts with a deep conviction about the values of customer centricity, quality and respect for individuals and then relentlessly pursuing them, creating a culture that promotes outstanding service.

3.18 How Can We Build a Culture Where Innovation Thrives?

Organizations around the world want to be innovative, but many of them focus on processes without paying adequate attention to culture, which limits their ability to innovate.

There are five powerful ways an organization can cultivate an innovative culture:

Mission that Inspires

A genuine mission to make a difference in the society inspires people, creating tremendous energy to innovate. Pursuing a powerful mission, employees innovate not because they are mandated to do so, but because they care about something bigger.

Integrating Diverse Talent

Innovative organizations consciously build a big pool of talent spanning a variety of expertise and diversity. For example, leading innovation-led companies like 3M and Apple thrive on bringing people with diverse talents such as those with expertise in science, computing, art, psychology and so on. And then they carefully nurture an enabling work environment to work together, creating possibilities to innovate.

Freedom to Experiment

Freedom to experiment is central to innovation, which implies a culture of trial and error and viewing failures as opportunities to learn. Supported by tools and processes, creativity flourishes when experimentation is a way of life for an organization.

How Can We Build a Culture Where Innovation Thrives?

Such organizations make it easy for employees to pursue their meritorious ideas.

Collaboration Across Boundaries

Creative people thrive in cultures where there is mutual respect for ideas, creativity and knowledge. They know that their contribution can follow different paths as not everything can be pre-defined including the teams they would be part of. Being comfortable with this relative ambiguity is normal in innovative organizations.

Rewarding Innovative Behavior

Good and inspiring rewards for innovative accomplishments send powerful signals to all the employees. Similarly, the way careers are managed is equally critical to managing creative talent.

The cultural attributes above may sound obvious, but in reality, a culture of innovation thrives only when *all* five of them are nurtured in an organization.

3.19 How Can a Culture of Trust and Transparency Be Built to Raise Performance?

Think of any well-known, successful tech company like Google, Amazon or Netflix, and you will be struck by one common theme: they all focus on building trust through transparency. Why?

Trust leads to higher levels of performance as employees push against aspirational goals without the fear of failure or embarrassment, pursue greater experimentation and hence more innovation. More importantly, an organization can attract high-quality talent that thrives in a culture of trust.

In such organizations, trust simply means employees are sure that nothing of significance is being hidden from them; they have a voice in the organization and expect to receive fair treatment at all times. While this may sound rudimentary, if an organization can achieve this level of trust, it has already laid the foundation for great performance.

Here are four good practices that build trust through transparency:

Openness in Communication

Communication is a powerful tool to build trust and transparency. It can take many shapes, from open-house meetings or all-hands meetings to frequent memos on a variety of subjects including strategic choices being made and explaining a point-of-view in impromptu, small groups. The underlying rationale is to let employees stay fully abreast of happenings without "hiding" any significant information and allowing two-way communication.

How Can a Culture of Trust and Transparency Be Built to Raise Performance?

Allowing Employees to Participate in Shaping Key Policies

Giving employees a sense of ownership of the decisions that affect their day-to-day life builds trust. For instance, many organizations poll employees or solicit suggestions on a variety of issues ranging from performance management, choice of rewards and other bigger issues to many others, such as choice of menu in the cafeteria.

Driving Performance Through Transparent Goal Setting Process

Transparent goal setting process drives performance-drives trust. As the process matures, it adds more trust. Trustworthy performance management system eliminates suspicion that often is a source of frustration. An organization can thus set aspirational goals and employees are encouraged to align their objectives with a similar degree of stretch.

Promoting Healthy Debate

Called "meritocracy" in many organizations, it implies that any group of employees/ team should always be encouraged to seek the *best* decision through a process of healthy debate. Disagreements would then be considered a part of the process. This is possible only when employees can be fully trusted to set aside personal prejudices and fully focus on the issue at hand. Trust thus builds healthy workplace relationships, paving the way for decisions based on merit.

If you decide to build your culture around the core value of trust, you have taken a huge stride towards building a culture of great performance.

3.20 How Can We Create a Culture That Supports the Digital Transformation of Our Organization?

From analytics, mobile strategy and cloud to social media strategy, machine learning and artificial intelligence— digital transformation may vary in its scope, but three distinguishing cultural attributes can pave the way for a smoother digital journey:

Humility at the Top

First, the leadership must show humility to accept that it doesn't know enough about the ever-changing digital landscape and its implications on the organization. Thus, leaders should be open to accepting "I don't know and need to learn." This kind of behavior leads to leaders themselves acquiring new knowledge, working skills and appreciating what needs to change, setting the tone for the rest.

Agility

As organizations connect to consumers directly through multiple channels, information flow is rapid and continuous, requiring quick analysis and response. Employees need to be organized (e.g. in autonomous teams), empowered and equipped with the required tools to analyze the information and act fast. In a world of instant transactions and feedback, decision-making needs a makeover as earlier time frames to analyze, think and act continue to shrink. Cultivating agility is an important step towards successful digital transformation.

Continuous Learning

Learning is central to embracing new technologies as well as integrating existing and new ways of working. Organizational

How Can We Create a Culture That Supports the Digital Transformation of Our Organization?

culture should encourage continuous learning as a way of life and employees at all levels should view adopting new technologies and skills as a core part of their roles.

A digital journey is as much about technology as it is about the mindset to accept change and learn. The three behaviors— humility at the top, agility and continuous learning— can create the right conditions for a successful digital transformation.

Exercise 3: Roadmap for a cultural change program

Step 1: Imagine the Opposite Future Scenarios

Think about the future of your organization, 3–5 years from now. Do you feel excited about the future or does it worry you? How would the future look if everything were to fall in place, the way you want? And what if things don't work out according to your plan?

The gap between these two scenarios represents the challenge for both strategy as well as culture; larger the gap, greater the challenge.

Example: Digital is a big opportunity. If we can embrace it, we might be at the forefront of our industry. And if we miss, we might just slowly become irrelevant. Not sure if we have the right culture to embark on such a make or break journey.

Now, describe these two scenarios:

Bright future: The exciting future scenario where culture can change to facilitate your vision.

_____

_____

_____

_____

Unwanted future: The scenario when the culture doesn't change and what it would lead to.

_____

_____

_____

_____

Step 2: Identify Business Challenges

Culture change always needs a context as defined by the business challenges. Bringing as much clarity as possible to these challenges is necessary. Challenges could be "problems" you are trying to solve or "opportunities" you want to ride.

Example: If one of the challenges identified was a decline in market share, then it needs a deeper understanding. Is it because of lack of product innovation? Is it because key customers are switching to an alternate technology? Is it poor service or prices, which are not competitive enough?

List out your business challenges:

1. _____

_____

2. _____

_____

3. _____

_____

4. _____

_____

5. _____

_____

Step 3: Review Your Culture

Turn your attention to the present culture: the mission, the values and behavior. Reflect deeply on your mission to understand its relevance to your vision. Now, focus on values and behaviors and divide them into three categories:

3.1 Dysfunctional Behaviors

Think of those dysfunctional behaviors that definitely need to change, as they are hurdles in realizing your vision. If they impinge on core values or assumptions, think deeply as to what change could really mean.

Example: We have poor accountability. Those in key positions get away in spite of covert opposition they mount to any new initiative. Seemingly poor performance gets rewarded. All this must change.

List them with some description:

1. _____

   _____

2. _____

   _____

3. _____

   _____

3.2 Missing Behaviors

Think of those values or behaviors that are largely missing (or are very weak) in the context of your challenges.

Example: We need innovation in good measure but have no idea what it means either in terms of talent, freedom, resources and processes. In the past, we have been talking about it, but our approach seems so risk-averse.

List them with some description:

1. _____

   _____

2. _____

_____

3. _____

_____

3.3 Facilitating Behaviors

Think of those values or behaviors that are your foundation and need to be nurtured all the time. You must seek opportunities to strengthen them.

Example: Respect for people is the foundation of how we work. But, it needs emphasizing all the time as it is key to deliver outstanding service to our customers.

List them with some description:

1. _____

_____

2. _____

_____

3. _____

_____

Step 4: Integrate Your Findings

The output of the above steps, when integrated, will give you a broad framework of what culture change entails in the context of your business challenges and what it would accomplish. Ensure your new set of ideas are consistent with the mission. This kind of process will get you started on a formal culture change journey.

Notes

Summing It Up

My purpose of creating this book was to provide senior leaders and practicing managers a practical and clear understanding of "what, why and how" of organizational culture, a critical factor that many organizations tend to overlook. I hope you enjoyed reading it and gained useful insights for uplifting the culture of your organization and its performance.

As you embark on a journey to focus on the culture of your organization, I want to leave you with some key questions for a deeper reflection:

- As an organization, do we have a unique identity?
- Do all our employees understand what we stand for?
- Are they relentlessly pursuing our vision?
- Can we trust everyone to behave and act according to our values?
- Is our culture evolving to keep pace with the future?

Ultimately, your own belief in the power of culture is central to how the organization at large would give importance and uphold your values. So, why not take some quality time to deeply think about it, in a small leadership group or even with peers and friends from other successful organizations?

Then, try to bring clarity to what culture *really* is? Organizations often mix up mission, values and HR practices as they grapple to define their culture. There could be pressure to manage public perception (e.g. website content, annual reports, etc.) or attract prospective employees (with slogans like "we are a family...") than to honestly state what your organization stands for.

Lack of a process to periodically review and reflect on culture (contrast this with well-defined strategy review sessions) at the Board and senior leadership level could be another dampener. If you can bring this simple discipline, over time, it will do a world of good. As a starting point, I would suggest organizations evaluate their cultural framework whenever they think of their business challenges or a new strategy or a higher level of performance.

On the other hand, if your organization is already enjoying the fruits of an enabling culture, I would suggest you don't fall into the complacency trap. Leveraging the sound footing, focus on future business challenges and how you may need to tweak the present culture to meet those challenges.

If you can truly recognize what culture can do to your organization's competitiveness and performance, rest is a matter of executing that belief. But it all starts with a single belief that culture matters!

Acknowledgments

A genuine word of gratitude for Edgar Schein, Professor Emeritus at MIT Sloan School of Management whom I have never met but I have accepted him as my Guru. His clarity of thoughts and wisdom are instrumental in shaping my own ideas on organizational culture. His practical insights are timeless and will continue to guide many generations.

Thanks to my wife, Abha, for having faith in my ability to write a book ("why don't you write a book?") and do much more. She has been a constant source of encouragement when things are good and when things are not so good.

Next, I would like to thank my younger brother, Atul, who sowed the idea of this book on organizational culture in my mind. He has been pivotal in structuring, editing and contributing with his thoughts. Thanks so much, Atul.

Lastly, through this book, a word of love for my children, Apoorva and Abhishek, who are trying to live up to my value of "simplicity at heart" in this complex world.

About Ajit Mathur

Ajit has a PhD in services management from Mumbai University, India, with an honors degree in mechanical engineering from National Institute of Technology (NIT), Jaipur and a postgraduate degree in industrial engineering from National Institute of Industrial Engineering (NITIE), Mumbai.

He has over three decades of rich corporate experience in a variety of organizations—leading Indian companies, a joint venture and a subsidiary of a global company. He was the Managing Director of Sky Gourmet, India, a wholly owned subsidiary of Gate Group, Switzerland. Earlier, he worked for the Taj Group, a Tata company.

Pursuing his passion for culture, he founded Right Culture, a start-up with a mission to help organizations achieve superior performance by taking ownership of their culture. He strongly believes that culture plays a pivotal role in shaping an organization's future and that leadership, in turn, should proactively shape culture.

He is based in Gurgaon, India.

www.rightculture.com

ajit@rightculture.com